Little Pebble™

## Construction Vehicles at Work

# DIGGERS

by Kathryn Clay

raintree
a Capstone company — publishers for children

Raintree is an imprint of Capstone Global Library Limited, a company incorporated in England and Wales having its registered office at 264 Banbury Road, Oxford, OX2 7DY – Registered company number: 6695582

**www.raintree.co.uk**
myorders@raintree.co.uk

ISBN 978 1 4747 2721 1 (hardback)
20 19 18 17 16
10 9 8 7 6 5 4 3 2 1

ISBN 978 1 4747 2725 9 (paperback)
21 20 19 18 17
10 9 8 7 6 5 4 3 2 1

**British Library Cataloguing in Publication Data**
A full catalogue record for this book is available from the British Library.

**Editorial credits**
Erika L. Shores, editor; Juliette Peters and Kayla Rossow, designers;
Eric Gohl, media researcher; Tori Abraham, production specialist

**Photo credits**
Alamy: B Christopher, 19, Frank Paul, 15; iStockphoto: Dr-Strangelove, 9, ewg3D, 21, gece33, 11, studio9400, 5; Shutterstock: Dmitry Kalinovsky, cover, 1, 7, lvto, 17, TFoxFoto, 13

Design elements: Shutterstock

Printed in China.

# Contents

# About diggers

Look!

Here comes a digger.

See the long arm?

It is called a boom.

boom

Booms go up and down.

The bucket digs and scoops.

bucket

Buckets have sharp teeth.

They break up big rocks.

teeth

See the big blade?

It is called a loader.

It moves soil.

loader

Joe is the driver.

He sits in the cab.

cab

# At work

A digger makes
a big hole.
Water pipes are put
in the ground.

A digger makes
land smooth.
Workers build
a new road.

A digger clears
trees and rocks.
Workers build
a new house.

Well done, digger!

# Glossary

**blade**  wide, curved piece of metal; the blade pushes, scrapes and picks up rocks and soil

**cab**  place where the driver sits

**smooth**  even and free from bumps

# Find out more

*Diggers* (Mighty Machines), Amanda Askew
(QED Publishing, 2011)

*First Book of Diggers and Dumpers* (Bloomsbury
Transport Collection), Isabel Thomas (A&C Black
Childrens & Educational, 2014)

*Noisy Diggers* (Usborne Noisy Books), Sam Taplin
(Usborne Publishing, 2012)

# Websites

www.ivorgoodsite.org.uk/
Meet Ivor Goodsite, and learn all about safe
construction sites.

www.toddlertube.co.uk/things-that-go/things-that-go-movies.html
The Things That Go! website has all kinds of videos
about construction vehicles, including several videos
showing diggers at work.

# Index